Mythologica

ILLUSTRATED BY RICHARD MERRITT AND SABINE REINHART

• EDITED BY HANNAH DAFFERN AND LAUREN FARNSWORTH • DESIGNED BY JACK CLUCAS • COVER DESIGN BY JOHN BIGWOOD •

The beasts in this book appear in the following order:

Minotaur • European Dragon • Jackalope • Basilisk • Gorgon • Cockatrice • Yeti
Pegasus • Ogre • Kraken • Gnome • Hydra • Harpy • Qilin • Kitsune • Unicorn
White Stag • Sphinx • Goblin • Griffon • Faun • Phoenix • Chinese Dragon
Mermaid • Troll • Werewolf • Fairy • Manticore • Centaur • Sea Serpent • Cerberus

First edition for North America published in 2017
by Barron's Educational Series, Inc.

First published in Great Britain in 2017 by LOM ART, an imprint of
Michael O'Mara Books Limited, 9 Lion Yard, Tremadoc Road, London SW4 7NQ

All inquiries should be addressed to:
Barron's Educational Series, Inc.
250 Wireless Boulevard
Hauppauge, NY 11788
www.barronseduc.com

ISBN: 978-1-4380-0952-0

Printed in China

9 8 7 6 5 4 3 2 1

BARRON'S

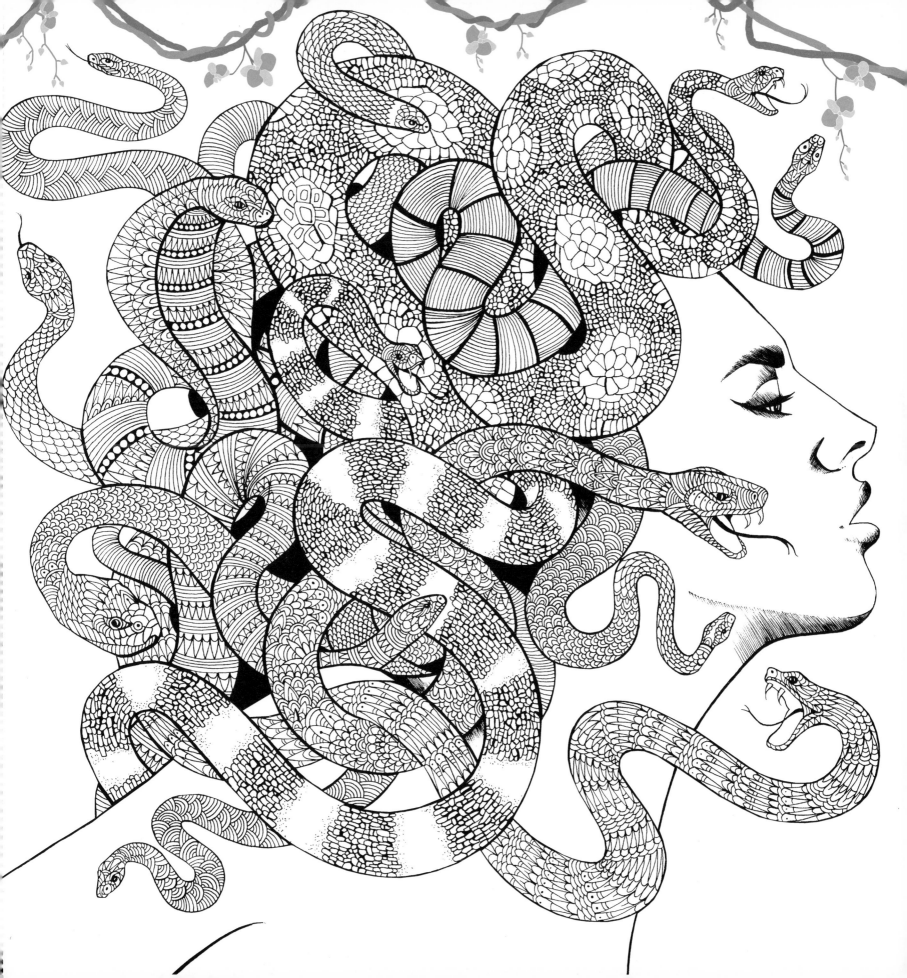